Table of Contents

Encouraging Interest

Help children to develop an understanding and appreciation for social and emotional learning themes through reading stories. A list of picture books is included in this teacher resource.

Blackline Masters and Graphic Organizers

Encourage children to use the blackline masters and graphic organizers to present information, reinforce important concepts and to extend opportunities for learning. The graphic organizers will help children focus on important ideas, or make direct comparisons.

Character Cards

Use the character cards provided as a springboard for discussions, role-playing, or to sort according to different emotions shown. Enlarge the cards while photocopying, and use them as a base for a bulletin board on social and emotional learning themes.

Role-Playing

Role-playing offers an excellent opportunity for children to become sensitive to how others feel in different situations, and to develop empathy. Be sure to introduce role-playing only after class members become familiar and comfortable with each other. In addition, set rules for role-playing to prevent inappropriate behaviour. For children to get the most out of role-playing, include the following:

- an enactment of the scenario presented
- a discussion and analysis of the scenario presented
- further role-playing of alternatives
- drawing conclusions regarding the scenario presented

Self-Esteem and Pride

Self-Esteem: to demonstrate a positive opinion of yourself
Pride: delight or satisfaction in your accomplishments, achievements, and status

Activity 1: All About Me

Have children celebrate themselves by filling out pages all about them! This activity is a great way for children to think about all the things they love, and what makes them who they are.

Activity 2: Student of the Week

Student of the Week is a great way to promote self-esteem and to instill pride. It will also encourage children to learn more about their classmates and to create a community. At the beginning of the school year, give families a specific week that their child will be Student of the Week. In preparation for that week, ask families to send in special photos such as baby photos to display, and a bag of items that the child would like to share and talk about with their classmates. Dedicate a bulletin board display with the child's information, photos, and school work. You may also wish to include written notes from the other children that compliment or recognize the child who is the current Student of the Week.

Activity 3: Celebrating Children

Acknowledge and celebrate children's accomplishments and positive qualities on an ongoing basis using the various certificates provided in this teacher resource. Keep track of which certificates have been handed to whom so you can watch for specific behaviours or accomplishments for certain children. Certificates can be given out in the moment, or you may wish to hold a regular class meeting to recognize children.

Activity 4: Perseverance

Have children set personal goals. Encourage children to persevere and to achieve their goals by

- affirming your confidence that they can achieve their goals
- giving honest feedback on what they are doing well and what they need to work on
- helping them break a task down into smaller more manageable parts if it seems overwhelming
- letting them know it is "okay" if something is not easy, and that they can work through it
- stressing the importance of "finishing what you have started"
- talking about your own experiences
- celebrating accomplishments and having children express how they feel when they achieve their goals

2

My Name Is...

_____

- -

_____

Here is a picture
of my family.

Here is a picture
of me.

My favourite colour is...

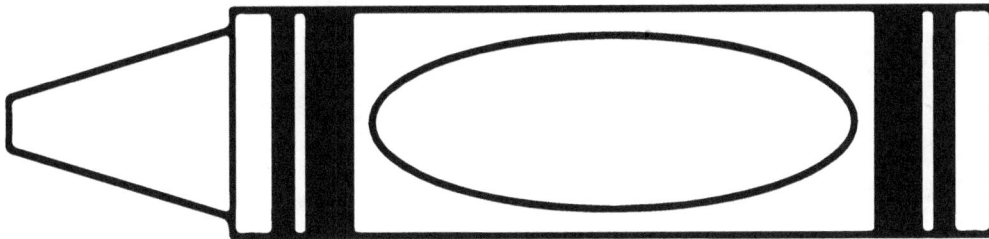

I am - - - - - - - - - - - - - - - - - - years old.

_____

My favourite food is...

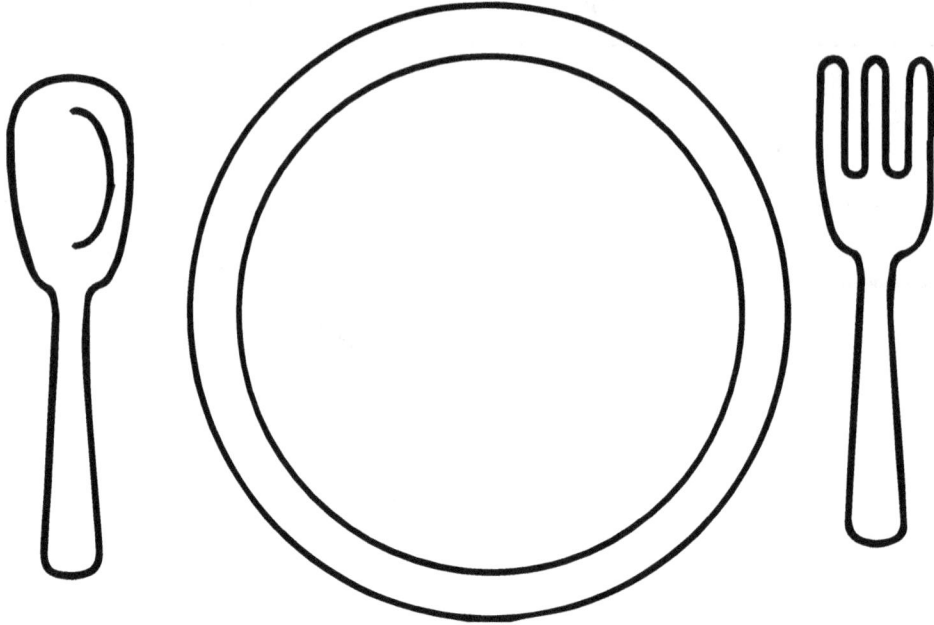

I live in...

_____

- - - - - - - - - - - - - -

_____

My birthday is on...

_____

- - - - - - - - - - - - - -

I love _____

- - - - - - - - - - - - - -

_____

I love _____

- - - - - - - - - - - - - -

_____

I love _____

- - - - - - - - - - - - - -

_____

My favourite season is...

This is what I want to be when I grow up.

My favourite animal is...

Draw or cut out pictures from magazines to create a collage that represents you!

Fill the spaces with all the things and people you love!

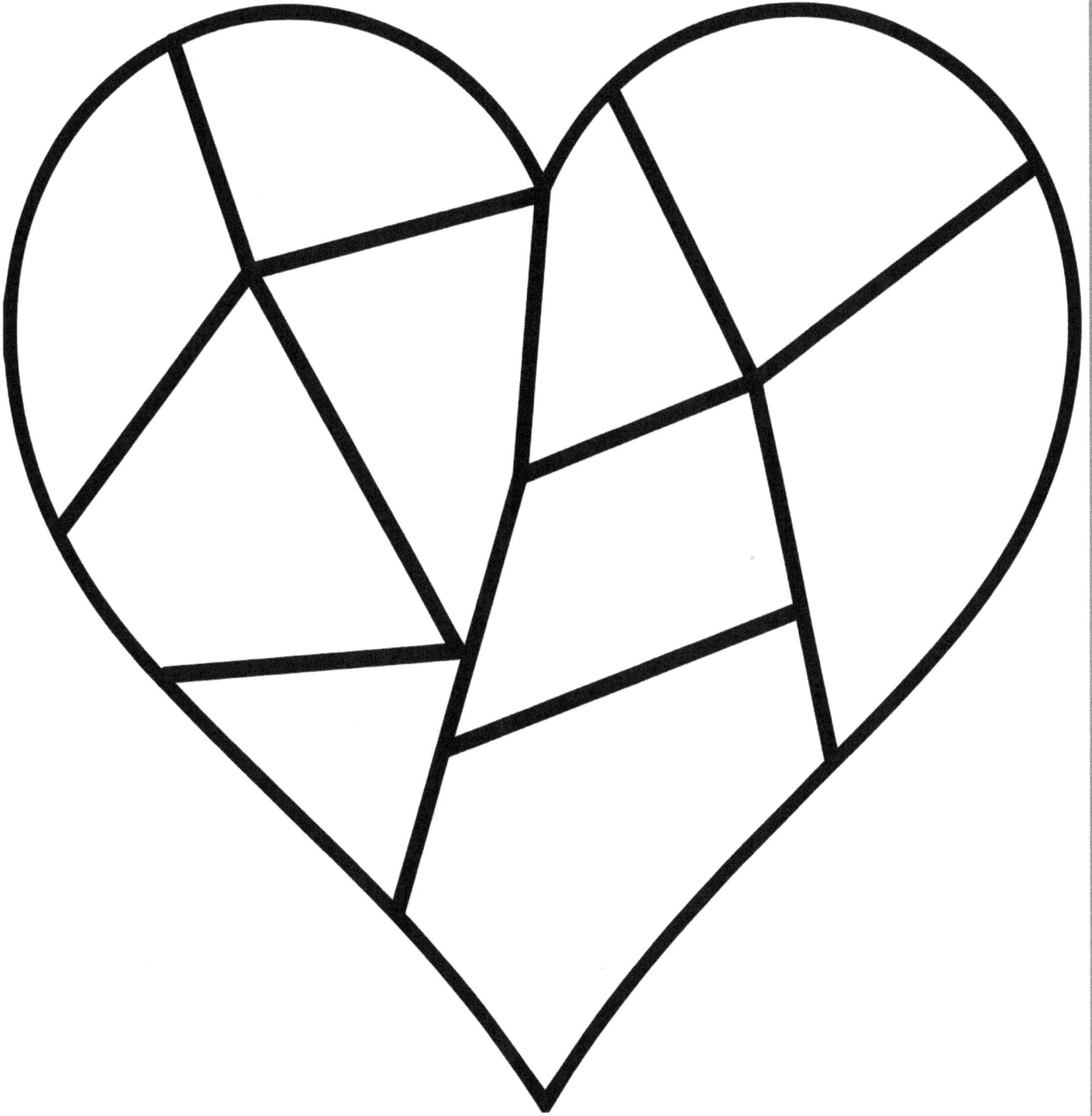

Student of the Week

Student of the Week: _____

Dear Parent/Guardian,

Your child has been chosen to be *Student of the Week* for the week of _____.
Please fill a paper bag with special items from home that your child would like to bring in to share with our class. Be sure to include photos of your child's choice for our *Student of the Week* bulletin board display about your child. In addition, please complete the information below to add to the display.

Your family's participation and support is greatly appreciated!

My favourite book is...

_____

My favourite food is...

_____

What I like best about school is...

_____

This is a picture of me.

My name is _____

Complete the sentence inside the balloon.

I AM PROUD OF...

_____'s Goal

To achieve this goal, I need to...

_____

- -

_____

I want to achieve this goal, because...

_____

- -

_____

My goal is to...

_____

- -

_____

_____'s

Book About Pride

I am proud when I learn how to do something new.

I am proud of
my work.

I am proud
when I win
at something.

I am proud
when I do well
at something.

I am proud
when I
conquer a
fear.

I am proud when I don't give up.

This is my drawing.
I am proud of me!

Empathy and Emotions

Empathy: the ability to understand and share the feelings of others
Emotions: A strong feeling that is often accompanied by a physical reaction.

Activity 1: People Have Feelings

Generate a class list of different kinds of feelings. Discuss situations that might occur around each feeling. Have children complete the Feelings worksheets and discuss their responses.

Activity 2: Caring People

Ask children, "What does it mean to be a caring person"? As a class, brainstorm a list of dos and don'ts for being caring. Ask for specific examples of each behaviour they identify.

Discussion Starters:
1. How do you think a new student feels when coming to a new class? What could you do to help?
2. What could you do to make a sad person happy?

Activity 3: Acts of Kindness

Brainstorm as a class what it means to be kind. Record children's responses on chart paper. Then go through the list children generated and have children associate the kinds of feelings they have around each act of kindness. Encourage children to understand that they have the ability to make someone happy, perhaps by complimenting them or doing something kind. Have children make compliment or appreciation cards for children in the class or create coupons to give out to people as an act of kindness.

Discussion Starters:
1. How does it feel to be kind?
2. How does it feel to be mean?

Activity 4: When People Feel Angry...

Ask children to remember a time when they felt angry. Have children explain what happened and how they handled the situation. Some situations might include

- something is unfair
- someone was mean or teased us
- something was broken
- someone is in our space
- someone is not sharing
- something has been taken away from us

Activity 5: Bullying

Help children gain a clear understanding of bullying. Bullying can be described as the act of hurting someone physically or psychologically. Children should also be made aware that bullies come in all shapes and sizes. Usually someone is bullied repeatedly. Some forms of bullying include

Physical: hitting, punching, tripping, shoving, stealing belongings, locking someone in or out, etc.
Verbal: teasing, put-downs, taunting, or making embarrassing remarks, etc.
Relational: excluding someone from a group, spreading rumours, or ignoring someone

It is the hope that if children can understand what a person feels like when bullied, children will develop empathy and help stop bullying.

Growth Mindset

The research of psychologist Dr. Carol Dweck tells us that people have two possible mindsets—a fixed mindset or a growth mindset. People with a fixed mindset believe that they are either smart or good at something, or they are not—and nothing can change that. People with a growth mindset believe that it is always possible to get better at doing something. Dr. Dweck has found that children with a growth mindset are more motivated to learn and achieve more than children with a fixed mindset.

How can you help children develop a growth mindset?

Talk about the brain: Explain that the brain becomes stronger by working hard to master new skills. Just as exercise makes muscles stronger, working at challenging thinking tasks makes the brain stronger.

View mistakes as learning opportunities: Let your child know that mistakes are valuable ways of learning where the problems lie. By carefully looking at mistakes, you and your child can learn where there are misunderstandings or missing pieces of knowledge. Mistakes pave the way to success!

Teach ways of dealing with frustration: Children can "turn off" when they become frustrated, which makes learning impossible. Teach your child ways to overcome frustration. For example, use the Internet to learn about breathing techniques that combat stress. You can also remind your child of skills that they have mastered in the past (such as learning to tie shoelaces) that took time and effort to learn.

Focus on praising the process: While it's fine to praise your child or the results they achieved, you can encourage a growth mindset by focusing your praise on the process. For example, praise your child's willingness to keep trying and their use of effective learning strategies such as asking questions.

Model a growth mindset: Look for opportunities to reinforce with your child how to see things from a growth mindset. For example,

If a child says…	Respond by saying…
I'll never get this!	Maybe you can't do it yet, but you'll get better if you keep trying.
I've been working at this for a long time and I'm still not getting it right!	Look at these areas where you've made progress. Keep working and you'll make more progress.
Hey, I can finally do this!	Let's think about how you achieved success. Some of the things you did this time might help you with the next challenge.

Positive Thinking

Cut out these cards and keep them handy. Use the cards for a positive boost anytime.

I do my best!

I train my brain!

I solve problems!

I don't give up!

I work hard!

I stay positive!

How am I Feeling?

Feeling	I feel this way when...	What I can do...
Furious		
Mad		
Sad		
Worried		
Happy		

How Am I Feeling?

curious

shy

excited

content

loved

frustrated

proud

joyful

lonely

pleased

silly

friendly

embarrassed

tired

outgoing

brave

How Am I Feeling?

happy

bored

confident

confused

disappointed

guilty

nervous

hurt

interested

jealous

angry

sad

scared

satisfied

surprised

thoughtful

21

How Am I Feeling Cards

Cut out the cards and use them to show different feelings.

Create a game of charades by randomly selecting a card, then having children act out that emotion. See how many emotions classmates can guess correctly.

sad

Draw your own!

_____

- - - - - - - - - - - -

_____

satisfied

scared

surprised

thoughtful

happy

guilty

confused

nervous

disappointed

hurt

interested

angry

jealous

23

© Chalkboard Publishing

curious

shy

excited

loved

frustrated

proud

lonely

pleased

silly

content

brave

embarrassed

joyful

tired

friendly

bored

outgoing

confident

_____

------------------------------ 's Feelings

I feel happy when...

I feel sad when...

I feel angry when...

_____
---------------------------- **'s Feelings**
_____

I feel excited when...

I feel scared when...

I feel brave when...

_____ 's Feelings

	I feel tired when...
	I feel proud when...
	I feel lonely when...

_____

- 's Feelings

	I feel silly when...
	I feel nervous when...
	I feel loved when...

Draw a line from the emotion to the matching picture.

sad

angry

curious

happy

loved

30

Emotion Match

Draw a line from the emotion to the matching picture.

confused

nervous

tired

surprised

excited

Emotion Match

Draw a line from the emotion to the matching picture.

scared

friendly

frustrated

silly

interested

Today I Am Feeling...

Draw how you are feeling.

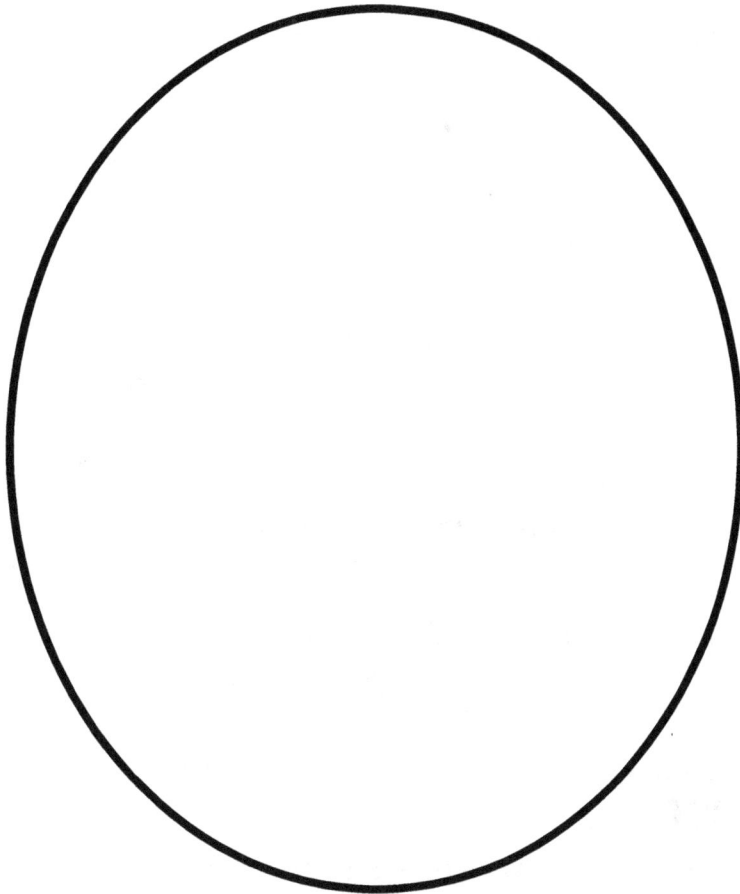

I feel this way because...

_____

- -

_____

_____

- -

_____

_____

- -

_____

Courtesy

Courtesy: being polite in attitude and behaviour toward others

Activity 1: Courtesy

Ask students if they know what the words *courtesy* and *polite* mean. As a class, brainstorm a list of courtesy dos and don'ts. Create a class big book based on the list generated by children.

Discussion Starters:

1. Why is it important to be polite to other people?
2. How do you feel when someone is polite to you?
3. How do you feel when you are polite?
4. How do you think others feel when you are polite to them?
5. Can you think of examples of how you can be polite to others today?

Activity 2: Encouraging Respect

Ask children what does it mean to treat other people with respect? Generate a class list of dos and don'ts for treating people with respect in different situations, such as when there is a class visitor. Post the list up on a wall as a reminder for children. Some of the dos and don'ts may include be courteous and polite, listen to others without interrupting, treat other people the way you want to be treated, don't give people put downs or treat them badly, and don't judge people before you get to know them.

Activity 3: People Are Alike

Encourage children to think about how people can be alike, but still unique. Survey children on a variety of topics and create whole class graphs to demonstrate how people can be similar and/or different. Some survey ideas include birthday months, favourite colours, number of people in their household, and favourite foods. In addition, celebrate the differences that children have.

Discussion Starters:

1. What do they notice?
2. What surprised them?

Activity 4: Friendship

Ask children to define friendship and if they think they have to be a good friend to have a good friend. Create a class "recipe" of behaviours for being a good friend. Discuss each one and have children name classmates who demonstrate each behaviour. Some behaviours might be someone who shares, is helpful, is kind, is fair, is fun, or is a good sport.

Discussion Starters:

1. I think the friendship behaviour I am best at is…
2. I think the friendship behaviour I need to work on is…

Courtesy Survey

People get along better when they are courteous to each other. Here are some ways that people can be courteous to each other. Take the survey and think about how courteous you are to others.

	Always	Sometimes	Never
I wait for my turn to speak.			
I use a tissue when I sneeze.			
I don't interrupt.			
I use polite words.			
I use good table manners.			

Do you think you are a courteous person? Explain your thinking.

_____

_____

_____

_____

I Can Be Kind

Draw a picture of how you can be kind in each setting.

This is how I can be kind in the classroom.

This is how I can be kind on the playground.

Acts of Kindness

Acts of kindness let people know that you care about them. Colour the boxes that are examples of acts of kindness.

listening

sharing your snack

being bossy

using manners

cooperating with others

including someone in a group

being helpful

being rude

teasing someone

_____'s

Book About Kindness

I am kind when
I invite someone
to join in.

I am kind when
I give someone
a helping hand.

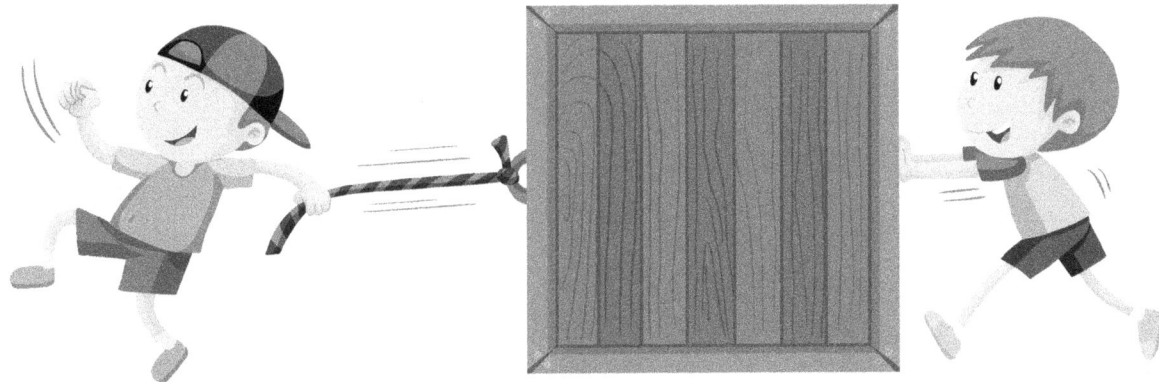

I am kind
when I talk
to someone
new.

I am kind when
I compliment
someone.

I am kind
when I use my
manners.

I am kind when
I listen and
don't interrupt.

This is my drawing of me being kind!

My Friend and Me

Here is a picture of my friend and me.

My friend's name is...

_____

- -

_____

We like to...

_____

- -

_____

Here is why we are friends:

_____

- -

_____

_____

- -

_____

Friendship Recipe

Here is a picture of my friend and me.

Write the ingredients that make a good friendship.

●

●

●

●

Write a friend's name in the box. Find a friend who...

has a pet dog	is the same height as you	likes to build things	has a summer birthday
has a sister	has a winter birthday	likes vanilla ice cream	likes to draw
has more than one pet	is wearing lace-up shoes	has a pet bird	likes the colour yellow
likes camping	has a brother	is an only child	likes to play outside

Friendship Survey

Friendship skills are very important. Here are some ways you can show you're a good friend. Take this survey and think about your friendship skills.

	Always	Sometimes	Never
I share with my friends.			
I take turns.			
I help my friends.			
I have fun with my friends.			
I am a good listener.			

Do you think you are a good friend? Explain your thinking.

_____

- -

_____

- -

_____

_____'s

Book About Being a Friend

Being a friend means sharing with others.

Being a friend
means having
fun together.

Being a friend
means being
there for
each other.

Being a friend means making each other laugh.

HA HA

Being a friend means trusting each other.

Being a friend means being helpful.

This is my drawing of me being a good friend!

Self-Regulation

Self-regulation: the ability to understand and manage your own behaviour and reactions

Activity 1: Establish a Calm-Down Corner

Create a calm-down corner or area in your classroom to provide a safe place for children to go to when they have a hard time controlling their emotions. Children sometimes need a designated space where they can take a break and regulate their emotions and bodies.

1. Designate an area: Select an area in your classroom where there is a low traffic, and children can comfortably go without disturbing their classmates.
2. Provide furniture: Create a pleasant space with pillows or a beanbag chair to relax on. If space allows, add a table or desk for children.
3. Include easily accessible resources. Here are some ideas:
   · calm-down tools that children can use to control their emotions
   · a poster to help children reflect and rate their "temperature"
   · a list of hands-on activities such as modelling clay and colouring pages
   · calming technique poster ideas
   · breathing prompts

Activity 2: Calming Strategy Cards

Use the calming strategy cards to reinforce with children that there are several available strategies to "cool down" when they are experiencing strong emotions. Talk with children about their feelings and which strategies might work best for them. Cut out the calming strategy cards, laminate and hole punch them to keep them on a binder ring. Alternatively, keep the strategy cards in a box readily accessible.

Activity 3: Glitter Jar

A glitter or "calm down" jar will help children relieve anxiety and stress. Simply, have a child give the glitter jar a good shake, then watch until the glitter settles back to the bottom of the jar. Watching the glitter settle will help a child to refocus and relax. Make a glitter jar by first filling a jar a third of the way with warm water. Second, add some glitter glue and stir until combined with the water. Next, add a few drops of food colouring. Then, pour in some glitter and stir until combined with the existing mixture. Lastly, top up the jar with more warm water while still allowing for a gap at the top to allow the mixture to move around. Hot glue the lid in place.

Activity 4: Mandala Colouring Pages

Help children relax by having them colour the mandala colouring pages found in this book.

Games That Encourage Self-Regulation

- Red Light, Green Light
- What Time Is It, Mr. Wolf?
- Relay Games
- Musical Chairs
- Simon Says
- Stacking Games
- Freeze Dancing

What's My Temperature?

5 — furious

4 — angry, mad

3 — sad, frustrated

2 — anxious, worried

1 — calm, happy, pleased

Calming Strategies

Cut out these cards to keep handy for when they are needed.

I can read a book.

I can blow bubbles.

I can do a puzzle.

I can phone my family or friends.

Calming Strategies

Cut out these cards to keep handy for when they are needed.

I can listen to music.

I can squish modelling clay.

I can push against a wall.

I can crinkle tissue paper.

Calming Strategies

Cut out these cards to keep handy for when they are needed.

I can pop bubble wrap.

I can have a dance party.

I can jump rope.

I can draw a picture.

Calming Strategies

Cut out these cards to keep handy for when they are needed.

I can kick a ball.

I can take 5 deep breaths.

1 2 3...

I can count to 10.

?

I can ask for help.

Calming Strategies

Cut out these cards to keep handy for when they are needed.

I can go for a walk.

I can watch my favourite movie.

I can drink some water.

I can write a story.

Calming Strategies

Cut out these cards to keep handy for when they are needed.

I can do a handstand.

I can sway back and forth.

I can think happy thoughts.

I can cuddle a toy.

Tummy Breathing

1 Lie down and place a stuffed animal on your tummy.

2 Breathe in deeply through your nose.

3 Exhale through your mouth.

4 The stuffed animal will go to sleep with the movement of your tummy.

Elephant Breathing

1 Stand with your feet wide apart. Let your arms dangle in front of your body. Interlock your fingers to make an elephant's trunk.

2 Breathe in deeply through your nose as you raise your trunk up above your head.

3 Slowly bend over at the waist and bring your trunk down. Swing your trunk back between your legs as you breathe out through your mouth.

Bubble Breathing

1 Sit with your eyes closed.

2 Imagine you are holding a bubble wand.

3 Breathe in deeply through your nose.

4 As you breathe out through your mouth, imagine you are blowing the bubbles into the room.

Balloon Breathing

1. Sit and place your hands around your mouth as if you were about to blow up a balloon.

2. Take a deep breath in through your nose.

3. As you breathe out through your mouth, spread your hands out as if you are blowing up a big balloon.

Shoulder Roll Breathing

1 Sit on the floor.

2 Take a deep breath through your nose and raise your shoulders up and roll them backward.

3 Breathe out through your mouth and lower your shoulders down and roll them forward.

4 Repeat slowly, rolling your shoulders up and down in time with your breath.

Bumblebee Breathing

1 Sit on the floor and place the tips of your pointer fingers in your ears.

2 Close your eyes and breathe through your nose.

3 Hum quietly as you slowly breathe out.

4 Do you hear a bumblebee?

5 Senses Breathing

1 Sit on the floor and breathe slowly.

2 While you breathe, find...

- 5 things you can see
- 4 things you can touch
- 3 things you can hear
- 2 things you can smell
- 1 thing you feel

Colour the mandala with your favourite colours to relax.

Colour the mandala with your favourite colours to relax.

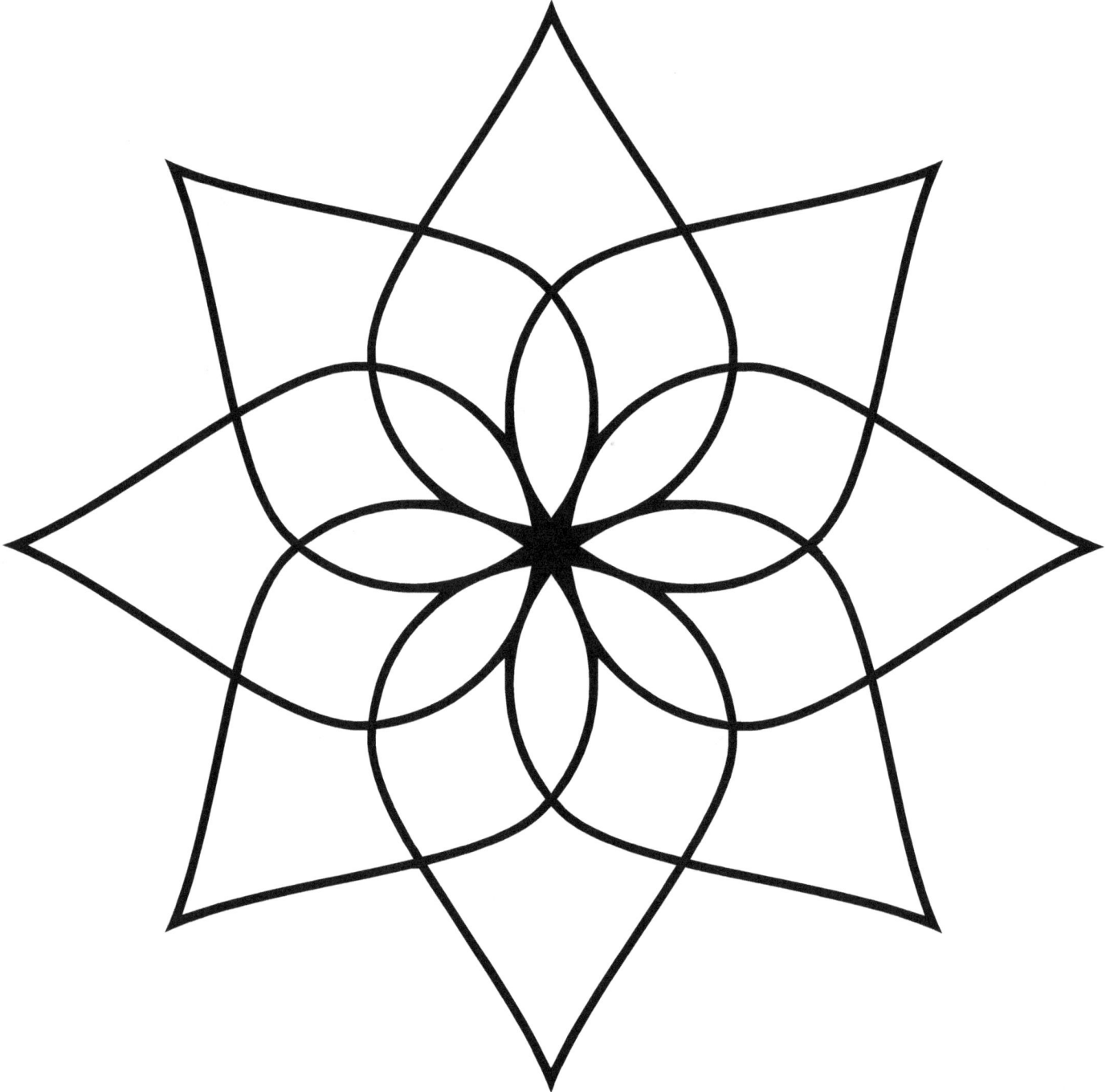

Colour the mandala with your favourite colours to relax.

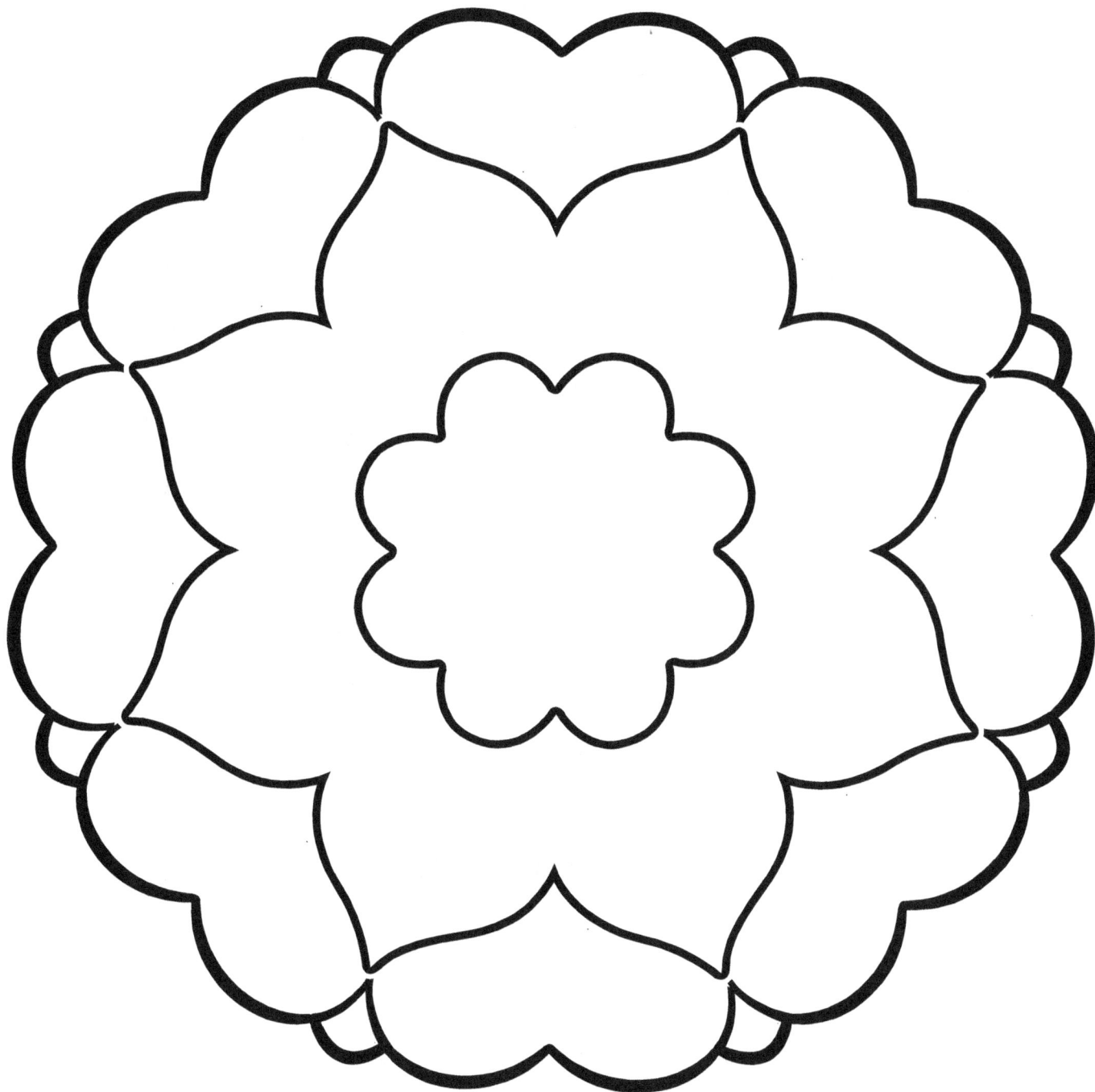

Colour the mandala with your favourite colours to relax.

Colour the mandala with your favourite colours to relax.

Colour the mandala with your favourite colours to relax.

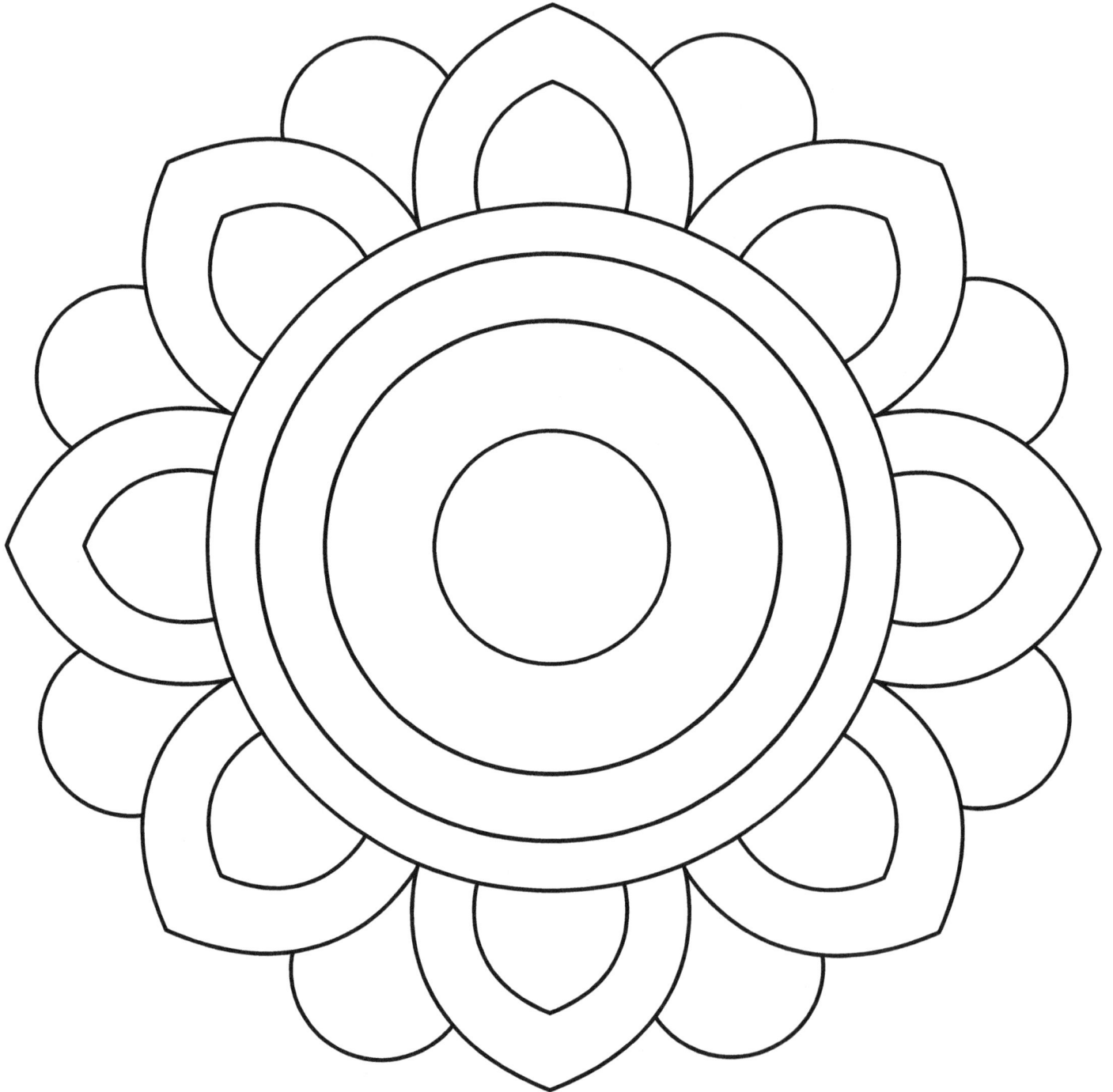

Fairness

Being truthful and just.

Activity 1: What Is Fairness?

Discussion Starters:
1. What does treating people fairly mean?
2. Have you ever said, "That's unfair"?
3. How do you know when something is unfair?
4. Have you ever played a game when someone cheated? How did you feel about it?
5. Does fairness mean enforcing the same rules for everyone, even if it means losing a game?

Activity 2: Honesty Is the Best Policy

As a whole group, ask children what they think the expression, "honesty is the best policy" means. Do they agree with the expression? Have children explain their thinking.

Discussion Starters:
1. Would you trust somebody who lies? Who cheats? Who steals? Why, or why not?
2. Have you ever told the truth, even though that was a difficult thing to do? Explain.

Activity 3: Making Good Decisions

Encourage children to learn to think about whether something is right or wrong before choosing how they will proceed in different situations. Role-play the different scenarios found on the good character cards in this book. Compare and discuss what happens in each scenario with children who choose to do the "right thing" and with children who choose to do the "wrong thing." How would they feel after each decision? What are the consequences?

Discussion Starters:
1. What can you think about before deciding if doing something is right or wrong?
3. What do you think would happen if nobody cared about doing the "right thing"?
4. Do you agree with "finder's keepers, loser's weepers"? Explain your thinking.

Activity 4: What Is Conflict Resolution?

Introduce the idea of conflict resolution. Conflict resolution is a process to help solve problems in a positive way. Each person involved is encouraged to take responsibility for their actions. For younger children, you may wish to refer to it as, "working it out." Clear steps for conflict resolution might include

- What is the problem?
- Listen without interrupting.
- Talk it out.
- Come up with different solutions.

Discuss and review the above process with children. Role-play different situations so children can practise walking through the process. Children should be encouraged to try to understand the other person's perspective in a conflict. You may wish to use situations that are reflected in their class. Encourage children to come up with different solutions so they get in the habit of trying to find another solution when one does not work. In addition, post the steps for conflict resolution on the board for easy reference for children.

_____'s

Book About
Fairness

Being fair means
taking turns.

Being fair means telling the truth and admitting mistakes.

Being fair means playing by the rules.

Being fair means thinking about how my actions affect others.

DO NOT LITTER!

Being fair means treating others how I want to be treated.

Being fair means everyone gets a seat.

This is my drawing of me being fair!

Being Fair

For each situation, colour the Yes or No if you think they are fair or not.

Somebody cuts ahead of you in line.

Is this fair?

YES   **NO**

Everybody takes turns swinging on the swing.

Is this fair?

YES   **NO**

Everyone got to put their name in the prize box.

Is this fair?

YES   **NO**

Somebody doesn't share any of the toys.

Is this fair?

YES   **NO**

One person takes two cookies when others got one.

Is this fair?

YES   **NO**

Someone drops money on the ground. You give it back.

Is this fair?

YES   **NO**

Problem Solving Techniques

Cut out these strategy cards and keep them for when things just do not seem to be going your way.

I can play with someone new.

I can say how I feel.

I can say "please stop."

please stop

I can leave.

I can ignore it.

I can ask for help.

Conflict Scenario Cards

CONFLICT SCENARIO CARD

The teacher has told you to line up for recess. Someone in the class pushes their way in front of you instead of going to the end of the line.

What would you do?

CONFLICT SCENARIO CARD

Someone in the class has taken your materials without your permission.

What would you do?

CONFLICT SCENARIO CARD

You are building a structure using construction materials and someone comes and knocks it down on purpose.

What would you do?

CONFLICT SCENARIO CARD

You and your friends are playing with a ball at recess. Another kid comes along and takes the ball away.

What would you do?

CONFLICT SCENARIO CARD

You and your and best friend get into an argument. Your best friend does not want to play with you anymore.

What would you do?

CONFLICT SCENARIO CARD

You are trying to do your work at your desk and the same person keeps bothering you.

What would you do?

Conflict Scenario Cards

CONFLICT SCENARIO CARD

One of your friends always makes you play the game that they want to, but they never play the game that you want to.

What would you do?

CONFLICT SCENARIO CARD

During basketball, a classmate yells at you and says you are not passing the ball to them enough.

What would you do?

CONFLICT SCENARIO CARD

You overhear a classmate saying mean things about one of your friends.

What would you do?

CONFLICT SCENARIO CARD

A classmate has told someone that you said something mean about them, but it was not you.

What would you do?

CONFLICT SCENARIO CARD

You and your friend both want to use the jump rope at recess.

What would you do?

CONFLICT SCENARIO CARD

A classmate said you cannot play with them.

What would you do?

Picture Book List

EMOTIONS

The Unbudgeable Curmudgeon by Matthew Burgess
The Way I Feel by Janan Cain
The Grouchy Ladybug by Eric Carle

COURTESY

Madeline Says Merci by John Bemelmans Marciano
No, David! by David Shannon

HONESTY / FAIRNESS

It's Not Fair! by Charlotte Zolotow
The Berenstain Bears and the Truth by Stan & Jan Berenstain
Alexander and the Terrible, Horrible, No Good, Very Bad Day by Judith Viorst

PRIDE

The Summer of the Swans by Betsy Byars
Captain Tom Cat by Bill Martin Jr
The Trumpet of the Swan by E. B. White

RESPECT

Goldilocks and the Three Bears by various authors
Grandfather Counts by Andrea Cheng

RESPONSIBILITY

Berlioz the Bear by Jan Brett
Now One Foot, Now the Other by Tomie dePaola
Horton Hatches the Egg by Dr. Seuss
Strega Nona by Tomie dePaola

COMPASSION

Berenstain Bears and the In-Crowd by Stan & Jan Berenstain
Frog and Toad Are Friends by Arnold Lobel
A Chair For My Mother by Vera B. Williams

FRIENDSHIP

Alexander and the Wind-Up Mouse by Leo Lionni
Best Friends by Steven Kellogg
The Invisible String by Patrice Karst
Hunter's Best Friend at School by Laura Malone Elliott

SELF REGULATION

Waiting Is Not Easy! by Mo Willems
I Can Handle It! by Laurie Wright
Sometimes I Feel Like a Storm Cloud by Lezlie Evans
Of Course It's a Big Deal by Bryan Smith

MANNERS

Manners by Aliki
What Do You Do, Dear? by Sesyle Joslin
The Bad Seed by Jory John
The Berenstain Bears Say Please and Thank You by Jan & Mike Berenstain

PERSEVERANCE

A Weed is a Flower by Aliki
Green Eggs and Ham by Dr. Seuss
Mike Mulligan and His Steam Shovel by Virginia Lee Burton
The Very Busy Spider by Eric Carle
The Little Engine That Could by Watty Piper

80

www.ingramcontent.com/pod-product-compliance
Lightning Source LLC
Chambersburg PA
CBHW081343090426
42737CB00017B/3276